KEEPING MY BALANCE

SPIRITUAL HELP WHEN SOMEONE I LOVE ABUSES DRUGS

CECIL MURPHEY

The Westminster Press
Philadelphia

Scripture quotations are taken from *The Living Bible,* copyright © 1971 by Tyndale House Publishers, Wheaton, Ill. Used by permission.

The book *Codependent No More* by Melody Beattie (Center City, Minn.: Hazelden Foundation, 1987) provides much helpful information and many insights for persons whose family members struggle with the problem of substance abuse.

Book design by Gene Harris

First edition

Published by The Westminster Press®
Philadelphia, Pennsylvania

PRINTED IN THE UNITED STATES OF AMERICA

9 8 7 6 5 4 3 2 1

Library of Congress Cataloging-in-Publication Data

Murphey, Cecil B.
  Keeping my balance.

  1. Family—Religious life—Meditations.
2. Co-dependence (Psychology)—Religious aspects—
Christianity—Meditations. I. Title.
BV4526.2.M87 1988   242'.66   88-191
ISBN 0-664-21877-6

CONTENTS

ONE

CARETAKING

KEEPING MY BALANCE

I felt as though I walked on a high wire as I tried to balance my life between other people and myself. On the one hand, I have obligations to them. Especially to her because she's my wife. They (and she) have a right to make choices, even when I don't agree.

At the same time I am responsible for my own needs. I've learned that taking care of myself is not as selfish as I once assumed; neither is caring for others as selfless as I once believed.

So I walk the high wire, struggling to balance the needs of others with my own. As I acquire greater skill at keeping my balance, I find life less threatening and more exciting.

God, help me keep that healthy balance so that I don't lean too far in either direction. Amen.

CO-DEPENDENT?

I was a co-dependent for years and didn't know it. I first heard the word *co-dependent* from a member of Narcotics Anonymous.

The term points to destructive emotional and behavioral patterns that develop from prolonged exposure to an oppressive way of life. Sometimes they emerge from our own character defects.

We co-dependents often become caretakers— not just caregivers. We tend to "take care of" the addict. Our own lives become unmanageable by living with and being committed to an addict. We make ourselves responsible for his or her needs.

For many of us, even if we get out of a particular relationship, we don't stay out. We soon become involved with others who have the same or similar problems. *But we can change.* When we recognize our co-dependency we take the first step toward our own health and our own recovery.

Mighty God, help me to break away from these dependent characteristics that bind me to continuous pain. Amen.

TAKING CARE OF ME

I didn't understand what it meant to take care of myself. People kept telling me I had to lead my own life and not let it revolve exclusively around his.

I tried to care for myself by selfish, demanding acts. I spoke up, often harshly, defending my actions with the words, "I'm only standing up for myself."

I used these words to force him into doing what I wanted and to deflect blame. I avoided admitting my anger. I imposed my will on him. "That's not my problem. I've got to take care of me," I said.

I woke up when I realized I was becoming indifferent to him and to everybody else. For me, "taking care of myself" promoted selfishness and unconcern. I'm trying to correct that. Taking care of myself doesn't mean ignoring others or being indifferent. It does mean not losing sight of my needs while I'm involved with others.

Loving God, keep me from getting totally wrapped up in myself. Amen.

CARING LIMITS

"I'll do anything to help her. Anything." I had come to the end. The therapist was my last hope.

"That's part of the problem," she said. "You're doing *everything*. You're protecting her and denying her the pain of struggling out of her own pit. You have to set limits to your caring."

I left in a rage. Who was she to say those things? If only she knew how bad things were!

Months later, I admitted she was right. I still care. I love my wife, but I'm no longer riddled with anxiety and compulsively rescuing her from every problem.

I'm solving my problems as they come. She's beginning to face up to her own. Even if she doesn't do anything for herself, I have set the limits of what I will do for her.

God, you won't do for us what we can do for ourselves. That seems obvious—now. Thank you for opening my eyes. Amen.

RELIGIOUS CARETAKING

I've been in the church since infancy. Yet I never recall a leader telling me, "You are doing too much." Instead I was always told to give. "It is more blessed to give than to receive" (Acts 20:35).

Sermons reminded us of Christ's unsearchable gift of life and how much God gives to us. We had countless examples of selfless givers and dozens of Bible verses to prod us on. We didn't examine our motives, believing that the needs determined the action. I envisioned myself as the good Samaritan who found the half-dead traveler on the road and nursed him back to health.

I've finally learned that caretaking doesn't work, in the church or in the home. I wasn't nursing people back to health, I was teaching them dependence. I helped prevent them from learning to fend for themselves.

Merciful God, forgive me for trying to ease pain by making people depend on me. Amen.

CONTROLLING LOVE

An oxymoron is a combination of two contradictory words like *dull shine.* Controlling love is an oxymoron too. The two words don't go together.

In the name of love I tried to push, pull, drag, nag, teach, advise, placate, and set straight.

When she argued (and she nearly always did), I backed off and sulked. "I was only trying to help because I love you."

I didn't have an addiction, so obviously I knew better than she did what she needed. I also felt that I had to stop her pain. If I didn't do it, nobody would. I knew I was right, and that meant she had to be wrong.

"I love her so much," I consoled myself. "I want her free." I did love her, but I didn't act lovingly. I acted like a benevolent dictator. And I wondered why I always lost.

Dear God, I'm learning to love by letting go. It's riskier this way, but I know it's right. Amen.

OUT OF CONTROL

I had daydreams about a spaceship out of control. I was the only one who could fly it. When others gave up I took over, and soon I had everything under control and we landed safely.

Those daydreams say a lot about me. I turned to them when I couldn't take his abuse of prescription drugs any more. I did everything I could to stop him, from direct commands to indirect appeals. I used guilt and my sense of helplessness; I threatened, argued, and cajoled. Yet in real life I never won. The more I tried to control events around me, the more I felt controlled. Thinking I knew how life ought to be, I wouldn't quit until I brought order from chaos.

I'm struggling to give up my need to control. At times it's frightening and I feel powerless. Now I can admit that I don't always know best.

Wise God, it scares me when I'm not in control, but it also tells me that I have to depend more on you. Amen.

DO WE COMMUNICATE?

When asked if we communicated, I said, "Yes. We talk together a lot."

That was true, yet our kind of communication involved both of us making one-way statements. We talked *at* each other. We sent messages all the time, but I don't think we received them.

I became an expert at sending messages of blame, threat, and coercion. When that didn't work, I begged and bribed. I dispensed advice, which she ignored. Sometimes I chose my words carefully to please her. At other times I chose them just as carefully to make her angry.

Things are changing. I spent years practicing all the harmful forms of communication. Now I'm learning to listen and to choose my words lovingly.

God, you're always trying to communicate lovingly with us. Teach me how to follow your example. Amen.

ABSORBED

I married him "for better for worse," and I've tried to live by that promise. I became so absorbed in his problems I seldom thought about my own—or even knew what they were. His bizarre behavior kept me off balance most of the time.

I cared about him. I cared too much. I can now acknowledge that at times I cared destructively by demanding and manipulating. It didn't work for him. And it didn't work for me.

A friend said, "You have been caring for him for so long you've forgotten how to care about yourself."

I've changed that. I care deeply about him and about his drug dependency and his other needs. Yet I can't help him by denying my own needs. If I am mentally, spiritually, and physically healthy, I can be of more help to him.

Wise and caring God, it does come down to learning to love ourselves first and then we can love others. Thank you for teaching me. Amen.

SHE'S DRIVING ME CRAZY

I told the counselor, "Our daughter skips school. She runs away. She's on coke and who knows what else. She sneaks out of the house after we're asleep. She does whatever she wants *when* she wants. And she's driving me crazy."

I had tried everything. I threatened, yelled, begged. I called the police, and she spent the night in juvenile detention. I tried gentleness and forgiveness. I once forced her into a teen drug and rehab center and she was fine, but only for a month. Nothing worked. "Why? Why is she doing this to us?" I asked.

The counselor gave me an answer that started me in the right direction. "First, we can seldom answer the why question. It doesn't make much difference anyway. Second, you can't control her, but you can gain control of yourself."

God, I love her and I want the best for her. Thank you for helping me to understand my greatest need right now is to get me *straightened out. Amen.*

SEX AND ALL THAT

Sex was a nightmare. For five years he had been so hooked on drugs that I had no feelings left for him. We would argue, and later one of us would apologize. The next thing I knew, he wanted to jump into bed and act like nothing had happened. I was still hurt and enraged.

For a while I did what he wanted, but I hated every minute. Later I found ways to avoid sex. Or I silently endured it. Sometimes I wished he'd die, or at least go away and never come back.

A few times I wanted to say, It would mean more if I just knew you loved me—and wanted more than sexual pleasure. But I couldn't talk about it. We never talked about sex.

Now that we're getting help and things are changing, I want sex to become an outward expression of our love for each other. I think he does too.

Caring God, help us to make sexual expression a loving act as you intended it to be. Amen.

SILENT RULES

I don't know how these rules started, but we obeyed them. They kept me confused and troubled. Here are five of them.

1. Don't talk about her problem. Keep a wall of silence around her.
2. Shut off your emotions. Speaking about feelings could ruin our family structure.
3. Never talk in direct terms about anything. We can lie by silence and partial answers.
4. Trust no one. We don't want others poking into our private affairs.
5. Never upset the delicate balance. We were always in danger of unplanned events that threw us into confusion until we could revert to our rules.

We no longer have these silent rules. We work hard to admit true feelings and even harder to express them. We try to talk directly about her drugs and how it affects us.

All-wise God, give us strength as we wipe out those binding, unwritten rules. Amen.

HIS MOODS

I tried to cure his bad moods, thinking that if he felt better, he wouldn't want drugs. When I sensed he was worried, I bolstered his self-confidence. When he was sad, I felt sad. I had a good day when he had a good day.

Although this happened on an unconscious level, his moods controlled my emotions. Then I, in turn, tried to control his feelings. I also tried doing it with our children, my parents, my friends. Everybody called me caring because I became so enmeshed in their lives I seemed to lose myself in other people.

I had no real life of my own and felt empty inside. It took me a long time to realize that I don't have to cure anyone's bad moods. I don't have to try to make others happy.

God, thank you for helping me to see that he has to cope with his moods and I have to learn to handle my own. Amen.

SHE'S GETTING BETTER, BUT . . .

I expected so much when she told me that she was getting help. "I'm going to lick this problem once and for all."

Eight months ago she started treatment at a rehab center, joined Narcotics Anonymous, read dozens of books, and listened to countless tapes. She got better and I should have been ecstatic. I wasn't. Her getting free of drugs didn't help me.

I felt used up, empty, useless. I felt rejected and worse than before.

"You have to get well too," one of her friends told me. That perceptive woman instinctively sensed my dilemma. "You've been in pain for so long you don't know how to feel good."

I've been learning that she and I have different problems but we're linked together. As she gets better, I am accepting help for me too.

God, it took me so long to understand how her problems affected me and my own peculiar brand of sickness. Thanks to you and my friends I'm better. Amen.

JUST DESERTS

I'd always heard about people getting their "just deserts." They only got what they deserved. I never heard that expression used when good things happened, but only in connection with lawbreakers or others who flaunt the rules of society.

For years I thought I got what I deserved by being married to a drug addict. I watched him ruin his life as he moved from Benzedrine to 'Ludes. The more involved he became with drugs, the more miserable I felt and the more I believed I was worthless. If I had been any good, I thought, I could have stopped him, changed him, encouraged him to quit, or talked him out of it.

I've learned differently since I've been to various self-help groups. It's not so much a matter of what I deserve, it's what I want and what I'll settle for. I've decided to settle for nothing less than being the best I can be.

Creator God, you created us to enjoy life. Remind me that you have so much more in life for me. Amen.

BETRAYED

She cheated and deceived me in every way. I put up with her behavior a long time. No matter what I tried to do for her, she let me down. I wanted to be a good and loving husband. Yet she twisted everything I said to use against me. She even lied to our friends about me.

One day when I railed against her betrayal, my sister asked, "What about *your* self-betrayal? You allowed it to happen." Although I was shocked, I needed to hear that. My wife had betrayed me, but I had helped. I cooperated in her destructive behavior. When I admitted that I had pinned all my hopes on her and then felt betrayed when she failed, I could see where I had to do some changing.

No matter how many ways or times she betrayed me, I let myself down first. Now I'm learning new ways to respond, both to her situation and to my own.

God, thank you for letting me see both sides of betrayal clearly. Give me wisdom, strength, and love to cope with her betrayal and *mine. Amen.*

A LIFETIME OF HABITS

I learned a lot of unhealthy habits in living with a man addicted to narcotics. Others learn these habits early in life, by growing up in a home with a parent addicted to alcohol or drugs.

One woman said, "At church I learned never to think of myself—only of serving and giving to others."

People, even fully normal, healthy people, can't live together without some disharmony. I, and other co-dependents, found it particularly difficult to live with addicted people. We formed habits to cope with outrageous circumstances. We did the best we could.

We learned these habits to meet our own needs in trying to cope with a complex world where no one handed us the rule book. Now we're outgrowing unhealthy habits. It takes courage and determination, but we're going to win.

God of mercy, you're helping me to change. Don't let me stop growing. Amen.

GIVING PEOPLE

I'm a giver. As a lifelong church member, I heard the message constantly held up as the ideal. Didn't Paul write, "God loves a cheerful giver" (2 Cor. 9:8)? Needy people attract me, and I want to do everything I can for them.

Yet nobody gives to me. Is this the way it's supposed to be? If I'm doing all this giving, am I the only one?

For the past few months I've been reexamining myself. This came about when I asked myself, If I'm such a giving person, why am I not doing something for *me?*

I'm also learning I can't take care of everybody. When I give myself to others—and especially to her, with her addiction problem—I have nothing left for me. At last I'm learning that I'm responsible for me.

Wonderful God, thanks for teaching me this simple but significant lesson. Keep teaching me. Amen.

WHO CONTROLS?

I figured out how to stop his pill taking—I stuck with him every minute. I gave him no opportunities to make connections. He still slipped out now and then, but most of the time I kept him in line.

I got so good I knew when he was ready for another high. I figured out all kinds of ways to divert him and turn him away from his addictive behavior—unless he got away from me.

Even when he escaped, I knew his hangouts and contacts. I went after him and usually found him high and wild. I brought him home and kept him out of trouble.

A friend asked, "Who's controlling whom? You're always there to grab him when he's in trouble and take care of him. He's got it made!"

I admitted it: she was right. He controlled me. That's when I knew I had to make changes, and the only person I could change was myself.

God, I don't want to control him any more. Or to be controlled. Help me to remember that. Amen.

WHERE'S MY CHEERLEADER?

"I've always been the cheerleader," Doug said. "I feel I started life as an adult, cheering on my parents. When do I get some one to cheer for me?"

Doug was telling my story too. I'd been leading the parade and cheering all my life. Once in a while I'd yell into the darkness, "Is there somebody out there to cheer for me?" I never got an answer. As Doug talked, I admitted that deep inside I felt that other people owed me a few cheers.

"Nobody owes you anything," a friend said. "If they want to give, fine, but we have to learn to cheer for ourselves."

The discussion helped me to grasp that others linked to substance abusers have the same needs and feelings. I had to break out of that mold of waiting on the sidelines for my cheerleader.

Loving God, you're my cheerleader, and I can cheer for me too. Together we're an unbeatable combination. Amen.

LEARNED PATTERNS

A friend dropped ears of corn into boiling water—still in their shucks.

"But aren't you going to shuck them?"

He shook his head. "This is the way we've always done it."

Both of us followed patterns we learned from our families. It was right because it was the way we learned through observation or experience. We seldom questioned the need for a better way.

My husband is addicted to narcotics, and I tried to help him for thirteen years. I blamed, complained, yelled, and did all the other unproductive things. I rescued him from his drug source, the courts, and the scrutiny of neighbors and co-workers. I never considered a different approach.

Only when I realized how I was following old behavior patterns without question did I seek new ways of coping.

Great God, show me how to cope and to learn healthy patterns of helping. Amen.

DID I DO THAT?

She's been clean for a year while I'm still struggling with guilt over all the destructive barriers I unintentionally put in her way. Now I'm facing what I did and learning not to repeat my mistakes:

- I did things for her I didn't want to do.
- I said yes when I meant no.
- I did things for her she could do herself.
- I took the initiative without being asked for help.
- Even when she asked for help, I did more than necessary.
- I spoke for her.
- I solved her problems.
- I never asked what I wanted or needed.

The list goes on. I now recognize my unhealthy ways of trying to help. I may still have a long way to go, but I'm learning.

Merciful God, thank you for showing me the truth about my behavior and for helping me to change. Amen.

PAY UP OR ELSE

He didn't show the first bit of gratitude when I pleaded in court for him. Because of me, he received a suspended sentence. I kept waiting for him to show his appreciation, but it never came.

Afterward I expected him to behave differently, and I told him so. At the time he agreed. "Anything. Just so I don't have to go back there."

Within weeks he went back to his old ways. I slipped in subtle reminders of his promise, but it didn't help. I hinted, then begged. I was getting nowhere.

That's the time when, as one writer expressed it, "we rip off our haloes and pull out our pitchforks."* I attacked him unmercifully for his callous deception and lack of gratitude. While my pay-up-or-else fury went to work, he responded with a silent I-never-asked-you-for-help attitude.

God, now that I am growing, I am also learning better ways of relating to him. Give me wisdom and strength to use this new understanding. Amen.

---

*Melody Beattie, *Codependent No More* (Center City, Minn.: Hazelden Foundation, 1987); p. 80.

YOU OWE ME!

I must have thought the words a hundred times. I did so much for her. I lost work and income. I paid her fines and pleaded for her with the courts. I almost became a recluse because of her.

Oddly enough, she didn't seem to consider that she owed me anything. Sometimes she didn't notice the trouble her problems caused me. She ignored me when I needed a little comfort.

You owe me! You owe me! I wanted to scream, but I knew it wouldn't change her. You're a taker! You expect me to give, give, give, and you won't do anything but take!

I know how foolish this sounds, but it made sense then. Instead of freeing her, I was trying to make her dependent on me. I'm glad now that the price for my help was too high for her to pay.

Generous God, remind me that she owes me nothing. Help me to give lovingly and freely without expectations. Amen.

HOW CAN I HELP?

When I was seven, our family moved. I wanted to do something, and I kept asking how I could help. "Just keep out of the way!" Dad yelled. I didn't see that as a positive answer.

Now I think of it differently. In coping with my addicted husband I wanted to help. Yet I didn't know the difference between good helping and harmful helping. I thought I was being a kind and faithful wife.

After his involvement with Narcotics Anonymous, I recognized that I helped most by keeping my hands off his problem. That may sound cruel, but I did as I was told. Less can be more. My withholding help sometimes makes me feel guilty, but it also offers more benefit than rushing to his aid.

God, I feel like such a slow learner, but it encourages me to realize that I am *learning. Amen.*

I ONLY WANT TO HELP

Our six-year-old dropped a dish and it broke. I screamed at her for being careless. Tears welled up in her eyes, and her bottom lip puckered. "I only wanted to help," she told me.

I had looked at what she had done and blamed her for what she had failed to do. I forgot—or ignored—that she intended to do good. She only wanted to help.

It made me think of my childhood and the times I suffered blame, criticism, and cutting words. Like my daughter—I only wanted to help.

By wanting to help, sometimes I did too much for my wife. Instead of freeing her, I sometimes did things that kept her enslaved to her addiction. Yet even the futile efforts came from the right motive: I wanted to help.

God, we want to do good things, but we go about it the wrong way. Give us wisdom to put the right acts with the right motives. Amen.

HELPLESS PEOPLE

"Of course he's helpless. Do you think anyone wants to depend on drugs to get to sleep? Drugs to get up? Drugs to keep going throughout the day?" I said. "He can't help himself."

"How do you know?" the counselor asked. I hauled out his list of failures for the previous two years to justify my point. The counselor held her ground. "You don't know if he is helpless or not. You never give him a chance."

I sheepishly admitted she was right. I had assumed he was helpless because of his addiction. And, if helpless, he needed me to do everything for him.

God, he's not as helpless as I thought. In some ways I've been more helpless, because I never pushed him into taking responsibility for his actions. Forgive me, God. Amen.

SHE'S GOT EVERYTHING

I wonder how many times I've fallen in love with a woman, thinking, She's everything I need. My mind and emotions endowed her with magical powers. She was the perfect mate, and having her would make my life complete.

I needed someone close and caring. Yet deep within I despaired of permanently attracting her because I felt unlovable.

I was wrong every time. I needed people and placed too much emphasis on someone else's providing emotional security and happiness for me. Because she couldn't be everything I wanted (and who could?), I felt rejected and even more unloved. Only when I stopped searching for a woman to make me complete did I begin to realize that completeness is an inside job.

God, I don't know all the reasons I searched for someone to take care of me. Keep reminding me that no human being can ever meet all the demands of another. Amen.

EASIER WAYS

In the nursing home they strapped my father down on his bed. "It's easier to keep him settled in," a nurse said with obvious pride.

"Easier is right! Easier for you! You destroy all his dignity and power of choice!" My anger spewed over the nurse. In time those words would haunt me.

Following my husband's serious surgery and lengthy convalescence, I found it easier to shove painkillers at him than to deal with my own discomfort as I saw his pain. "He shouldn't stay on Percodan," the doctor warned me. Yet when he begged, I gave in.

I now realize that's how I used to relate to him. I took the easy route of solving, changing, or yielding rather than letting him face his own problems.

God, help me not to settle for the expedient and ignore the necessary. Amen.

TOO LITTLE

I'm a needy person, and I've been aware of that most of my life. I yearned for that superhuman woman who doesn't exist, and I kept searching for her.

In desperation, I finally turned to a woman who responded to me. I couldn't have all I wanted so I settled for too little. I constantly complained about her flaws.

"Why do you stay with her?" people asked.

"I love her," I said, and yet I couldn't think of one reason why. Life with her was filled with one problem after another. Peace became only temporary before a new onslaught of trouble.

That's when I knew I was stuck. I was afraid to leave because I didn't know where to go or how to stand on my own. So I stayed. And we have both been miserable.

God, you promised a rich life, but I settled for emotional poverty. I need your help as I pull myself out of this pit. Amen.

IN THE WRONG PLACES

I wanted love and approval like everybody else. I don't recall my parents ever complimenting me. They just complained when I didn't do a good job.

I sought love—but I looked in all the wrong places. I went after men who couldn't love me in return. I never asked if they were good for me or if I could be happy with them. I jumped into relationships whenever I met men I thought would make me happy. They never did.

Now I'm married to a man addicted to prescription drugs. His addiction consumes most of his energies. Yet I had expected him to love me and to make me happy.

Now I know a secret. I can never find happiness in another person. I've looked for love in the wrong places because any place outside myself is a wrong place. I have to like me first.

Teacher God, remind me often of your love and that I can truly love myself and be happy being me. Amen.

CARETAKING AND CAREGIVING

I never thought of the difference between caretaking and caregiving. I was the former; I'm learning to be the latter.

Caretakers take over for others. They make the decisions. They control. They dominate. They also say "I'm doing this for your own good" and believe their words.

As a caretaker I felt anxious and guilty and tried to anticipate her needs before she asked. I didn't mean to do all that. I wanted to help and to show I love her. I never planned to take care of her like a nurse.

Caregivers offer love and help but refuse to do for people what they can do for themselves. They accept responsibility for their own actions and refuse to cover up for a loved one. They support them as they struggle with how to live.

As a caregiver I'm learning to let her do for herself what only she can do. Then I support her decisions.

God, you care without caretaking. Help me learn from your example. Amen.

THE CLASH OF WILLS

I tried to impose my will on him for a long time. I demanded he leave his pills; I tried to force him to my way of doing things. Our wills clashed, and I lost.

I've changed since then. I've turned to God, but I still bump up against a clash of wills— mine and God's.

For a time I uselessly groaned, "I shouldn't be this way." Now I'm learning that God and I don't always see things the same way. That doesn't make me the bad guy. It only reflects my imperfect understanding. I'm not discouraged either. I keep learning new lessons about the clash of wills.

Most of all, I've learned to pray.

God of grace and power, I give you my preferences. I accept your choices. Amen.

DYING DREAMS

The words of our wedding vows promised "for better for worse." I meant them when I stared into her eyes and said them. I naively assumed that "worse" meant transitory moments and "better" described the norm. Our life together reversed that concept.

I had dreams of togetherness and a supportive relationship. Slowly those dreams died through one disappointment after another. This wasn't the life I had envisioned, the romance I had in mind, and I didn't like it!

It took years, but a part of me died. So what happens now? That's where the pain hurts most. The woman I love is controlled by a hunger for drugs, and my dreams have eroded —slowly but thoroughly. I want to stay with her, but I wonder if it's too late. Then I vow that, with God's help, I'm going to give it my best shot. I'm going to get better even if she chooses not to.

Healing God, you know the inner pain I face. Help me resolve it by choosing what's best for me. Amen.

FRIENDLY UNHELPING

I used the term "taking care" because I thought it expressed a high degree of concern and showed that I wanted to help her with her addiction.

Caretaking sounds like a friendlier act than it really is. To take care of her implied incompetence—she couldn't do it herself. If she couldn't help herself, I reasoned, she needs me.

I didn't understand (or perhaps couldn't, because of my commitment to caretaking) that many times people only do for themselves when no one else will.

Because I never forced her to take care of her own needs, she leaned on me. Once I realized my friendly unhelpfulness, I made efforts to get us both out of our respective positions.

God, I want to help but I don't want to do too much. Let my helping lead to her growth rather than hinder her progress. Help me to be a caregiver instead of a caretaker. Amen.

TWO

EMOTIONS

FEELINGS COUNT

"You're too emotional," she accused me. From then on, I stored my feelings in the deep freeze of repression.

"Don't you have any feelings? Are you a zombie?" she screamed. That day I tried to thaw out my feelings, but they were too deeply frozen.

A lot of things have taken place since then. I know now that feelings count. I can't always depend on them because they're volatile. And I don't want them to control my behavior.

Yet my emotional side is special. If I freeze it, I lose an important part of me. My feelings express joy and sadness, fear and peace, anger and contentment. I allow my feelings to indicate (not dictate) how things are going in my world. They help me understand myself better.

God, I'm thawing out my emotions, and most of the time I like being able to feel again. Help me value this important part of me. Amen.

WHO'S SICK?

"You're sicker than I am," she said. "Who wouldn't be a druggie, living with you? You're the sick one!"

Those words hurt and I lashed back. I had stood up for her, apologized for her, made excuses, even hidden her addiction. Yet I knew she was partially right. In my own way, I was sick.

One therapist called me passive-aggressive. "You hold out a loving hand, and when she takes it you kick her in the shins." He helped me to see that I hindered her recovery. He helped me to admit that my hindrance was a sickness too—a different kind from hers but just as real.

I am learning to look honestly at myself. It's not easy to say, "I am a manipulator. I make demands and I'm hostile. I work by subterfuge." Only by admitting my form of sickness could I get better.

God of all kindness, help me see my own sickness before I point my finger at hers. Amen.

A FAMILY DISEASE

The woman started her speech by saying, "Drug addiction is a family sickness." Anger flooded over me. My husband was the one who went outside our home, got hooked, and made us suffer.

When I probed more deeply, I grasped what the speaker meant. Addiction does affect all of us in the family.

We inadvertently conspired with him by telling ourselves that we were a family and we'd stick together and work it out. It tied us more fully into his addiction and hooked us into the game of cover-up, denial, anguish, guilt, and all the other symptoms of the family disease.

As long as I concentrated on faultfinding, I couldn't admit I needed help. When I took the spotlight off him and faced my own needs, our family was ready for help.

Loving God, thank you for helping me see this as our family in need and not just his problem. Amen.

MAKING IT GO AWAY

I wanted her problem with drugs to go away. I kept saying, "If she'd just quit taking those pills, we could be a normal family." I demanded and I blamed. "After all," I reminded her, "it's your problem. You brought the chaos into our home. When you get rid of your habit, we can be happy again." But that approach doesn't work.

Someone told me addiction is like catching a cold. When one family member catches it, before long the other members are infected. That's when I woke up. She has the drug problem but I've been infected too. I have no trouble with drugs, but I'm part of the problem. If I want change to occur, I'll have to do something for myself.

"I have a problem too," I finally said. I sought healing for myself. I learned to look at my attitudes, feelings, and behavior. I am on my own road to recovery. I hope she will fully recover too. But regardless, I must get over my own infection.

All-powerful God, I know that problems won't just go away. Thanks for helping me to face them. Amen.

OF COURSE I'M ANGRY!

Why shouldn't I be angry? We had a normal home like everybody else. He spoiled it with his abuse of prescription drugs. I warned him. "You're taking too many," I said. "You're going to get hooked." He never listened.

As his dosage increased, so did my anger. Why is he doing this to me? Why can't he just leave the junk alone?

A friend helped me to admit that I felt more than anger. I was hurt and scared, ashamed of him and of being linked with him. I didn't realize I lived with a man who was also hurt, scared, ashamed, and angry.

Unconsciously, I let my anger overwhelm me so I couldn't feel my pain. At times I wondered if I would ever *not* be angry. Once I understood that most of us who live with addicted people have similar emotions, I didn't feel so alone, guilty, and ashamed. Because I'm getting help, I'm no longer angry all the time.

God of all truth, thank you that I'm getting better every day and in every way. Amen.

NO ANGER NO WAY

I don't know why I never questioned it, but the tacit rule in our family was, "We do not get angry."

Here are seven reasons why those of us who live with drug-addicted people insist on holding to this foolish code of "No anger no way."

1. It's wrong to feel angry.
2. Anger accomplishes nothing.
3. Good people don't feel angry.
4. We lose control when we get angry.
5. People will dislike us and reject us.
6. Getting angry means I don't love you.
7. Getting angry is sinful.

All seven reasons are untrue. I'm slowly learning to express anger in healthy ways. I'm determined to be a healthy individual, and healthy people experience the whole gamut of emotions, including anger.

God, help me to express my anger in appropriate ways. Amen.

THE JOY OF ANGER

Does it sound strange to link joy and anger together? For years I never felt anger. I cried. I hurt. I felt lonely. But I never experienced anger.

Actually, anger was there—disguised as something else. Because I didn't shout or pound my fist, my anger didn't show.

I have since realized that anger controlled much of my life. Hostility lurked below the surface, seeking ways to sneak out. My looks and gestures gave me away to others. One friend said, "Just walking into your house, I can feel the vibrations of rage."

Because I believed it was wrong to get angry, I never admitted its existence. Now I know this was more self-deception. I was angry, keeping the emotion rigidly controlled—and denying a large part of myself in the process. Once I started to get better, I also faced the reality of my anger. I still have trouble expressing it, but I'm getting better.

God, help me face the reality of my anger as a human part of me. Amen.

"YOU'RE SURE ANGRY"

She often called me angry and hostile. I countered with, "Putting up with you would make anyone angry."

I talked with a friend, and, as usual, I went on a tirade about her latest drug episode. When I paused, he said calmly, "You're sure angry. I suspect your anger keeps you from being totally crushed. It's your defense weapon."

That had never occurred to me. I had often blown up, reminding myself that anyone who tolerated what I did had a right to rage. "You don't have to be angry," he said. "You can't stop her from doing what she wants. It's her life. But you don't have to live in a state of perpetual anger."

I've since realized how my anger worked. It was my way of screaming at the unfairness of life. In my chaotic world I used anger as my defense. It also prevented me from looking at myself and my own needs.

Caring God, I hid behind anger a long time. Now I seek your freeing power. Amen.

TRUST?

"I mean it this time," he said. "Trust me." I wanted to believe him, but I had been down that path too many times.

I couldn't believe anything he said. Over the years he had failed so often I couldn't trust him. Worse, I couldn't even trust my own judgment. I would determine not to put up with his behavior or give him another chance and then end up by giving in.

I couldn't trust my feelings. I wondered, Am I the sick one? I'd make decisions with no confidence I'd done the right thing.

It seemed that when I turned to friends, they let me down. I was sure God had abandoned me. I was alone and couldn't trust anyone.

When he started therapy, the therapist told me, "I want to help you to trust." I have been learning to trust others and to trust my own feelings. From that beginning, I am now digging out of my black hole.

Faithful God, you never left me, but I hurt so badly I didn't know that. Thank you for the people I can lean on in my weakness. Amen.

MY GUILT

I put a lot of effort into being a good husband and father. I followed all the rules. I devoted my life to my wife and children, even turning down two fine job opportunities because I didn't want to disrupt the family with a move.

Yet I always felt guilty—about everything. When our son became addicted, I felt guilty because I couldn't cure him. I felt guilty when I couldn't do everything my wife wanted, when I didn't live up to others' expectations or to my own rigid standards.

Maybe I'll always have to struggle with guilt, but I'm getting help. Now I know I don't have to be perfect or conform to strict rules and behavior patterns.

Perfect God, when I insist on being a perfect parent or husband, I'm trying to be like you. Help me remember you're the only one who's perfect. Amen.

GO AWAY, GUILT!

I used to feel guilty over everything. Our daughter cut her leg and I assumed guilt for not being more watchful. I felt guilty because I wasn't at the hospital when Mom died. If he got high, guilt gnawed at me for not preventing it. When he lost his job—a regular occurrence—I blamed myself for not being more supportive.

Once I had wound the cords of blame around myself so tightly, it took a long time to start getting free.

I still feel guilt—often. So I yell, "Go away, guilt!" One time I ran to the back door and kicked as hard as I could, symbolically chasing unwanted guilt away. I'm learning to undo a lifetime of habitual unhealthy emotion.

God, thank you for relieving me of guilt. I'm learning that I haven't done as much wrong as I once thought. Help me as I continue to kick false guilt out of my life. Amen.

I CAN'T HELP THE WAY I FEEL

I took on the job of caring for her needs, feelings, actions, choices, well-being, and ultimate destiny. When she had problems or her addiction seemed worse, my emotions raced to anxiety, panic, or guilt. I couldn't rest until she felt better. I compulsively tried to make it better for her.

"You shouldn't be doing all this," friends advised. "You're killing yourself."

"But I can't help the way I feel," I said. I now admit that while I can't help the way I feel, I can change the way I behave. I can override my emotions to do the wise thing. My feelings are beginning to change. I feel less responsible for her problems. I yearn for the day when I can say and mean that she is fully responsible for her needs.

Faithful God, you've brought me so far. Help me continue to choose my behavior instead of reacting from feelings. Amen.

HURT FEELINGS

I didn't want to hurt anyone, especially him. I bent over backward in speaking kindly and in sweet tones. I protected him from my own rage, never exploding like some wives I've heard about. I didn't let him put himself down either. I encouraged him and remained patient in his angry moods.

Do I sound like the model wife? Don't be misled. I didn't want him hurt, but I ended up hurting myself. I stopped trusting my own feelings. I worked hard at keeping my tongue under control. I showered him with kindness and cheated myself out of the quality of care I lavished on him. While I saw his need for less condemnation and more compassion, I couldn't turn around and give those things to me.

Now I tell myself, "I don't have to protect him. I can be good to myself and appreciate my human feelings." I can admit it when I hurt and not hide behind forced smiles.

God, thanks for soothing my hurt feelings and for being there. Amen.

MY SHADOW SIDE

I didn't like a lot of things I was feeling, so I did something about them: I denied them, like most men I know. It's safer that way, and it doesn't hurt so much.

I pushed away rejection and pain. Yet I sensed that, deep inside, I was an angry man and I didn't like that. I didn't like other things about myself, and I tried to hide them from me.

One day I heard about the need to face "our shadow side"—the anger and pain and other parts of me I didn't like. As I admitted anger, resentment, hatred, loneliness, and rejection, I hurt. For days I agonized with the pain and even wanted to die.

Over a period of months my support group helped me to accept my shadow side. "That's part of who I am," I finally said. By accepting my dark side, I diminished its power and moved to a greater sense of wholeness.

God, thank you for helping me face my shadow side. It helps me define who I am. Amen.

WHY DO I FEEL SO BAD?

I'm getting better. I'm less manipulative, less demanding, and less angry. I'm also more focused on my needs. Yet why do I feel bad so much of the time?

I think it's because I am a rescuer, a savior. I find fulfillment in saving others. That sounds noble and good. But we savior types aren't content to rescue. After we rescue, we persecute. We dictate. We control. We say, "I'm protecting him from himself."

Eventually we end up as victims. It's like wrapping your arms around a drowning person. Then we make heavy demands. When they don't respond (lack of positive response for us means rejection), we feel like victims. And the cycle goes on.

I've broken the cycle. My actions are ahead of my emotions right now. At times I lapse back into bad feelings. That's when I remind myself, "I'm doing the right thing."

Caring God, encourage me as I move in the right direction, even though I still have occasional bad feelings. Amen.

KNOWING

If you ask, I can tell you everything he's done or didn't follow through on. I can tell you what he thought, felt, and said, or I can reverse it and tell you what he *didn't* think, feel, or say. I knew how he ought to behave. After all, we have rules about normal living.

Ask him, and he'll tell you that no one understands him the way I do. I can look at him and almost read his mind.

Friends marveled at my uncanny ability. And yet I didn't have any insight into my own life. As long as I focused on his problems, I hid truths about myself from myself. One day I asked, "What good does this do for me?"

Listening to the answer helped me to get in touch with *my* needs. I hurt. I felt lost and unwanted. In facing my own problems, I learned to be more effective as his wife and helper.

All-knowing God, help me see myself more perfectly—and especially my own needs. Amen.

CUTTING OUT THE BAD

I wanted all the positive emotions of joy and love. I hated the bad feelings and determined to get rid of them. I hid my anger behind a smile, my resentment behind my silence.

I couldn't cut out the bad feelings. If anything, they grew bigger. Trying to cut out the bad is like cutting moth holes out of a piece of cloth. It only makes things worse.

Emotional withdrawal can lessen our negative feelings, but we lose the positive ones as well. By denying my negative emotions, I was losing the ability to feel intimacy, love, peace. I enjoyed nothing.

When I got help, I had to acknowledge those unacceptable feelings along with the good ones. Being a whole person demands it, and I wanted wholeness. Each day I'm getting healthier by facing all my feelings.

God of all emotions, help me to feel the way you intended. Give me what I need in order to cope with the downside of my emotions. Amen.

JUSTIFYING MY EMOTIONS

I didn't like my emotions—especially how I felt toward her when she was messed up with pills. When I felt bad, I immediately found a reason: She won't listen to me. She won't do anything for herself. I'm tired after having stayed up with her half the night. She disrupted my day.

I've learned a lot of things in recent months about my feelings. Emotions are morally neutral. How we *use* our emotions determines the good or bad result.

I've learned to say, "I'm angry. I hurt. I resent your words." I'm trying not to justify my emotions. If the feelings are there, I acknowledge their presence.

My goal now involves two steps. First, to feel the emotions without denying their existence. Second, to choose what to do about the way I feel. Previously I exploded with rage or sulked from rejection. Now I can choose how to react.

God, I'm in charge of directing my response to my emotions, and I need your constant wisdom. Amen.

INVITING EMOTIONS

I had been feeling so bad for so long that I couldn't take any more depression. Our pastor told me, "You're stuck in one feeling mode. You're going to have to learn how to unstick yourself."

When I didn't understand what he meant, he said, "Invite emotions into your life. You don't have to shut off your emotions. Welcome your feelings—all of them. They are a vital part of you." He taught me to pray for my feelings to become obvious to me and to invite them into my consciousness. "Treat them gently," he urged, "and don't be afraid of them. Trust them when they come."

I still pray the prayer he taught me:

Loving God, I invite my true feelings to emerge today. I commit myself to accept them and to care for them. Amen.

WHO SAYS SO?

I never realized how tightly I held on to her. I justified my actions by saying, "She needs me. I don't have a choice."

When people suggested I loosen my hold, I recoiled. "I couldn't do that! I love her too much. I have to do this for her."

One wise friend shook her head. "Who says so?" she asked.

That simple question started me moving in a new direction. I began the first steps toward what the experts call detachment. I slowly moved away from living her life for her and worrying over everything she did. It wasn't easy, but it was right.

Wise God, thanks for forcing me to answer "Who says so?" Thanks even more for the strength to detach myself from her addiction. Amen.

DELUSIONS AND ILLUSIONS

Control is an illusion; it doesn't work. It only seems to. When I played the role of police officer, he conformed. Not changed, only conformed. When I dropped my guard, he did exactly what he wanted to do. I couldn't control either his pill taking or his behavior.

He sometimes punished me for trying to help. Instead of being grateful, he lashed out at me, yelled, and publicly embarrassed me. Sometimes it seemed as if he doubled his efforts to prove to me that he could go on doing whatever he wanted. I finally accepted my delusion. No amount of control brings about a permanent or desirable change in another.

God, I don't want to delude myself any more. I care, but I don't want to control. Help me to know the difference. Amen.

BURN IT UP

One day an old school friend was coming for a visit. My wife was so high she didn't talk sense. When something like that happened I used to yell, "You let me down again, and you knew how important this was to me!"

This time I reacted differently. The house was a mess and I raced through the rooms, cleaning and vacuuming, beginning in the den where my friend would come in. I jogged to the bakery and the deli and had our food ready.

By the time my guest arrived, I no longer felt angry. I felt tired, delighted for a chance to sit down and relax with him.

That's one way I cope with my anger: I burn up the energy through physical activity—*quite aware of what I am doing*—instead of using it on anger. I've used this helpful method many times. I admit my anger first and then seek creative ways to burn it up. For me, it works.

God, help me appropriately to burn up unpleasant emotions as I face my feelings. Amen.

AFTER ALL I'VE DONE

Our church helped a financially troubled family to stay together. Yet they never visited our congregation. One member growled, "After all we've done for them, they don't even come to worship here."

Did we try to buy them by doing good for them? If we acted kindly to get something from them (their attendance), were we truly kind or helpful?

Those of us who live with addicts know well this conditioned giving. We help, and if they don't respond the way we expect, we're hurt, angry, and resentful.

We do too much, but we want something out of it. We ignore our own needs, then feel hurt when they don't appreciate our sacrifices or take our advice.

Their lack of proper response can force us to rethink our tactics. That, in turn, can lead us to realize that doing good to get rewarded seldom works.

Giving God, teach me to give the way you do—freely and without condition. Teach me to give from a full and loving heart and not from anticipated gains. Amen.

VICTIMS' VICTIMS

"Why? Why? Why?" I tortured myself. I had started by rescuing him and ended up feeling victimized. I had played that scene so many times I could have written the script in advance.

Then one day while I was viewing a film on incest, the voiceover said, "Many of these perpetrators were themselves victims of incest."

The words had an impact like a heavy fist against my chest. I understood. I had been a childhood victim. My alcoholic parents neglected me, verbally abused me, and sometimes beat me. I had started the cycle in childhood of trying to take care of them and being punished for my efforts through violence.

For the first time I felt hope. Aside from my husband's own addiction problem—probably the reason he attracted me in the first place—I was replaying my childhood script. But I didn't have to stay with those stage directions. I could make my own.

God, help me overcome those childhood patterns and be his supporter, not his rescuer and torturer. Amen.

ANOTHER COMPLETED CYCLE

I couldn't decide if I was more angry or hurt. I had given so much and she had rejected my efforts. I felt sad and helpless. Self-pity oozed from me. "What good does it do to help people? They thank you by kicking in your teeth. I've been used again." As I heard myself say the word *again* I grasped that I was caught in a repetitive cycle.

"Will it always be this way?" I asked a friend.

"Only as long as you keep trying to take care of her," he said.

I realized that my life had been a series of cycles. They all started with high hopes and ended with dashed dreams.

"Only you can put words to the tune you sing," he said.

I'm now singing new lyrics and breaking the cyclical pattern. It's better for both of us.

Thank you, loving God, for teaching me that with your help I can break the power of the terrible cycles. Amen.

I'M NOTHING ALONE

A best-seller title stated it clearly: *Why Do I Think I Am Nothing Without a Man?** You have a man you're not happy with—in my case, an addict. You want out of the relationship. At the same time, you honestly don't think you can live without him. You need some man.

A truer way of saying it (and I learned this recently) is, "I don't believe I can take care of myself. I don't know if I want to take care of myself. I need somebody to be there for me."

I've also learned I don't have to live that way. I am growing and, with God's help, I can survive happily without depending on him or anyone else.

God, it's hard for me to face being alone and not to rely on someone else. Keep reminding me that you're with me so I'm never truly alone. Amen.

---

*Penelope Russianoff (New York: Bantam Books, 1982).

DUTY CALLS

"Nothing stands above duty." I don't recall that anyone actually said that, but I grew up living by that creed. Duty meant my taking responsibility for everyone in the family. If they hurt, I had to heal. I had to discover the cure for every sickness.

I got so good at responding to crises, I anticipated the call of duty and could even rescue in advance. After all, who knows better than Dad what each person needs? I was the one who must supply.

As a good husband, I tried to cope with everything, no matter how serious, or I felt inadequate and useless. It took a long time to hold back and to ask, instead, "What do you want from me?"

God, I'm pleased that I'm asking the right question. Help me to hear the need before rushing in with the solution. Amen.

AFTER THE UPS

He's better and has stayed off drugs for months. He got a promotion at work. I felt great, almost euphoric. Everything seemed so wonderful.

Then I got scared. *What's going to happen next?* I started to prepare myself for disaster to strike. That's how my life used to operate. I hated to feel good because it signaled the prelude to chaos. I also believed that I didn't deserve to be happy.

I'm moving away from such negative mind-sets. *I deserve happiness.* It's okay to feel emotionally up. When sad times come, I'll accept them as well. But an avalanche of trouble doesn't have to follow the snowflakes of joy.

God, I'm no longer afraid of feeling good. You created me to have positive feelings, and I know it's all right. Thanks for making that possible. Amen.

THE REAL MESSAGE

We co-dependents are good at deciding what other people think. We interpret every nuance of phrase or gesture, even though we're not always accurate.

We're harder pressed to interpret ourselves. Yet if we're going to move forward, we have to learn to feel our own emotions without blocking them or trying to change them.

When we're uncomfortable with what we're feeling at the moment, we can pause and examine our emotions. I've found it helpful to ask myself, "What's the real message here? Tell me what I need to know now about myself."

Maybe I need to calm down before I do anything. Perhaps I'm afraid of the consequences of the feelings. We can usually find out by inward probing for the real message of our emotions.

God, help me know what my feelings are trying to tell me. I get confused easily so I need your help. Amen.

THE WAY IT'S SUPPOSED TO BE

I had devoted myself to seeing that my husband beat his drug problem. I did everything I could think of. Yet my emotions got stirred up—"If I'm helping, then why all this uneasiness inside me?" I felt guilty for not doing more. Guilt plagued me when my good intentions didn't succeed.

I felt, This is not how it's supposed to be. When I help another, I'm supposed to feel good and so is he!

Friends helped me look objectively at the situation. I had tried to make both of us feel and act "the way it's supposed to be." They helped me abandon that useless concept. "Accept life as it is. Listen to yourself and to God. You can't program feelings or control results. Don't let your self-giving be destructive." Now I'm concentrating on listening before I act.

God, I'm listening to my inner voice. Help me hear clearly. Amen.

RESCUING AND OTHER BAD WORDS

"What's wrong with being a rescuer?" I yelled. "If I don't help, who will?"

"But who are you rescuing? And why?" a friend yelled back. "Are you saving your wife from herself or creating more problems?"

Since that initial conversation, I've heard the word *rescuer* linked with *caretaker* and *enabler*. All these words have a similar concept. When we assume responsibility for another person, we are rescuing. Later we become angry at them for what we've done and feel they used us for their needs.

In this context, enabling is a destructive form of helping. Enabling took place when I did anything that helped her to continue her drug habit. I enabled when I shielded her from the consequences of her actions. I help more when I let her do things for herself. I know all these truths, yet I still find it difficult not to intervene.

All-wise God, you are the only rescuer, and you didn't appoint me to assist you. Amen.

ACTORS AND REACTORS

Someone has said there are two kinds of people in the world: those who make things happen and those who allow things to happen.

I'm in the second category. Instead of taking initiative or responsibility for myself, I let things happen and then I react. I waste my energies going around putting out fires that somebody else has lit. We reactors let others fire the initial salvo before we rush into action. We overreact or underact, but rarely act. We respond to others' problems and pain. We react to their addictive behavior.

It's not easy for us to initiate change or to assert ourselves in making choices. But it can be done, and some of us are learning how.

God, help me as I move away from acting in response to what others do. Amen.

THREE

RESPONSIBILITY

HER PROBLEM

She's got the problem and I've got her. That's how I tried to distance myself. I didn't take drugs but I felt victimized by her drugs.

When she rambled on about hitting high states and rising above problems, I hurt and didn't have the anesthetizing benefit of drugs. I hurt because I cared and suffered my own kind of agony.

I constantly worried: How will she do today? Will something throw her off track? I found help when a speaker pointed out that we who love addicts hurt and our pain is just as real. She said, "Addicts numb their feelings and nonabusers double over in pain."

I needed comfort, care, and help. I suffered in the background—until my pain hurt so much I had to get help *for me.* Now I'm getting it and feeling better.

Loving God, thank you for helping me see that it's more than her problem. I need to find comfort from you and from other caring people. Amen.

RESPONSIBLE

All my life I've felt responsible for taking care of someone. If anything needed doing, they asked me. They depended on me. I was a good daughter, a fine sister, a dependable mother.

When something went wrong, I accepted it as my personal responsibility to straighten out or solve. I healed the wounds and stopped the fights.

I never thought of how unhealthy I made the situation. His constant use of drugs meant he refused to take responsibility for his own actions, so I compensated. He felt so little responsibility; I felt so much. I know now that trying to carry the whole load doesn't work. I won't do for him what he can learn to do for himself.

God, you hold me accountable for my actions, but only for my own. Help me remember he's accountable for his own, too. Amen.

RESPONSIBLE FEELINGS

Responding appropriately makes me accept the responsibility for my emotions. I can't make myself feel or change the feelings. I can't blame my moods on anyone else.

I tried to blame her for making me upset. "You ruined my day!" I scolded. "You keep me upset over your stupid pills." I made a lot of charges to avoid self-examination.

I got better when I finally figured out the simple link between my emotions and my mind. What I think can influence my emotions. When I think I am being taken advantage of, I start to feel bad. If I decide she said the words to hurt me, pain and rejection come to the surface. I'm now reexamining my thinking. By getting my thoughts straight, I can influence how I'm going to feel.

God, help me think responsibly so I can move more positively toward my emotional well-being. Amen.

RESPONSIBLE FOR ME

I'm responsible for me. I've heard that for years, and now I'm learning what it means. Part of my self-duty lies in providing me with the best care of which I'm capable.

I've made a list of the things for which I hold myself accountable. I am responsible for:

- What I do to him and to others
- What I allow others to do to me
- My own desires
- My needs—emotional, spiritual, physical, and social
- What I give and what I receive
- Defining and achieving goals

No problem solvers can take away my areas of stress. I have to solve my own dilemmas or learn to live with them.

This understanding comes from a basic fact: I count. I am important to God and to myself. Now I know that, I can cope with life and accept my responsibility.

God, grant me wisdom to give myself the good care I need—and deserve. Amen.

DISGUISED EXCUSES

"Why do you put up with it?" his sister asked me. "He treats you badly, and I don't think he'll get any better."

"He needs me," I said, too quickly. I didn't put it into words but I meant, He couldn't survive on his own. I did add, "I married him, and after all, I have some responsibility for him."

"If you ever get tired of playing the martyr role," she said, with kindness in her voice, "there is help for you out there."

I couldn't follow her advice for a long time because I kept disguising my excuses for taking care of him. Only when I stripped myself of those delusions was I ready to change.

Loving God, help me put away the self-deceptions and false excuses. Amen.

IT'S HIS FAULT

I didn't care what happened to him. I had gotten him out of one scrape after another. He made the messes, and then I had to chase around with a broom and sweep them up.

"You caused all our problems," I yelled. "If it weren't for your addiction, we'd have more money, a better home. Bills wouldn't pile up. But you don't ever think of anything except feeding your drug habit!"

He had his problem with drugs, but I was a victim too. I didn't see that until after he joined a local Narcotics Anonymous group. I've since started to think differently. He has a problem. He'll probably always have to battle against addiction. I have my own problems— just as serious in a different way. I judged harshly. I blamed. I focused on his faults. Now that I understand, I've been getting help for me.

Compassionate God, it's easy to tell you the ways he failed this week. Forgive me for keeping score. Make me more understanding and less blaming. Amen.

THE CAUSE OF IT ALL

"The reason I take pills is because of your nagging," she yelled. "You're the cause of my problems!"

In reflection, I considered what she had said. Was I *the* cause? *A* cause? Or was I simply making normal responses to abnormal situations? Did I want to be needed so much because it was the only way my life held meaning? I finally saw some truth in her charges.

I didn't cause her problems, but I finally admitted that my attitude and actions did affect her. I had become entwined in her addiction. I have also learned that I didn't have to remain alone in my torment, guilt, and pain. I found supportive help in Narcotics Anonymous, and, relying on God's strength, I'm growing and assuming responsibility for my own behavior.

God of hope and help, thanks for being there when I needed you and for sending caring people into my life to help me face my own problems. Amen.

MOVING THE BOUNDARIES

When I first became aware of his problem, I set the limits. "I won't tolerate this again," I said. I meant those words. Yet within three months he did all the things I said I would never tolerate. And I ended up doing things I said I never would—such as covering up and lying for him.

I felt hurt. Used. Unloved. Worse, I kept allowing myself to be hurt again and again. Eventually I went the other way, where I tolerated nothing.

Neither approach helped him or me. I had to have help—and I got it. I also had to learn just where to set the boundaries—and not to yield.

When I enforce the boundaries, I don't always feel good; sometimes I feel cruel and unloving. But I know I'm doing the right thing, for him and for me.

All-caring Creator, you set limits for your creatures and you hold us to those limits. Give me the strength to know where to hold the line for him. Amen.

REPEAT PERFORMANCE

On TV I saw a 1947 film about a woman who shot a man and then had a chance to relive the last year of her life—knowing what she had already done. At the end of the year (the second time around) she shot the same man with the same gun. The movie, appropriately enough, was called *Repeat Performance*.

That's how I've lived for most of my life. I kept repeating by finding new people and situations, but the relationships all ended the same way. Almost as if foreordained (I once said), every woman who has seriously attracted me has been, in some way, chemically dependent. "I have a gift for picking the wrong women," I once said bitterly. Now that I recognize my compulsive attraction for these drug-dependent types, I'm changing inside. No more repeat performances for me!

God, I've diagnosed the sickness. Give me strength to apply the remedy. Amen.

SAYING NO

I had trouble saying no to him. When I managed to say no and stick to it, guilt ate away at me. I had rejected him. Or he might reject me.

More than just saying yes, I did things I didn't want to do for him and constantly found ways to justify my caretaking. I had lost confidence in my ability to make wise decisions. I had so little self-esteem that I allowed him to twist me around and confuse my thinking. Afterward I told myself how I should have stood up, should have argued, but I didn't—for a long time.

It's still hard to say no. I struggle with guilt, with failing him, coping with his accusations that I'm mean and uncaring. Yet I'm getting better at asserting myself. I know that I can make decisions and keep them—even if I have to shout "No!"

Dear God, thank you for helping me learn when to say no and how to stick to it even if I feel guilty. Amen.

PROGRESSIVE

"It gets worse," the therapist said. "You start with a little concern over her sickness. As she progresses, you get sicker in your own way."

I didn't believe him. Not then. In time I learned. Chemical or substance dependency is progressive. The more intense her condition became, the more intense my own.

She got worse and I got worse. I felt more depressed, isolated, and confused. I had wanted to help her so much, and I felt helpless. Knowing that I probably contributed to her problem made it hurt more. A few times I considered suicide.

Now I am getting help in facing my life, my abilities, and my human limits. I've stopped my progressive descent.

God, you want me better and you've helped me. Don't let me stop or be satisfied. Amen.

LOVING ME?

Why should anyone love me? I couldn't do anything right, always said the wrong thing, and failed constantly. I wasn't good enough to like.

I wanted love and acceptance but, believing I couldn't have them, I settled for being needed. That's not enough any more. Reading *Another Chance: Learning to Like Yourself** inspired me. Finally I've begun to love myself in a healthy, sensible way.

I realize I have value simply because God created me. God loves me just as I am—even knowing all my failures and mistakes. Each day I help myself by repeating two statements: *I am of value. I like being me.*

One day I had to say them out loud for ten minutes before they sank in.

Loving God, remind me that you endowed me with worth and loved me when I couldn't love myself. Amen.

---

*See Cecil Murphey, *Another Chance: Learning to Like Yourself* (Philadelphia: Westminster Press, 1987).

WILL I EVER CHANGE?

"Can I change? Will I?" I asked that question often. I prayed for a miracle to change me. I didn't know how to do things differently.

The experts convinced me that I was so busy responding to her problems, I didn't have energy to identify and provide for my own needs. I could do nothing to change her. But, they said, "You can do some things for yourself."

I worked at it—worked as hard at changing me as I had previously done in trying to change her. Yet the doubts came. Can I change? Can I learn healthy ways of achieving? In the beginning I got discouraged because I kept slipping back into the old comfortable but unworkable patterns.

Now I do things differently and I *am* changing. I have begun a process, and I don't plan to stop.

God of help and guidance, thanks for the miracle that makes me know I can change— and I am changing! Amen.

ADAPTING OR ACCEPTING

I faced a crucial question. Was I adapting or was I accepting his attempts to free himself of his drug dependency?

Adapting means giving up, resigning myself to things the way they are. That includes feeling sorry for him and tolerating aberrant behavior.

Accepting means I face the changed circumstances of our relationship. He is different now, a man I hardly know. Accepting means I have to make changes too. I have to face my powerlessness to control his actions.

As he grows, I have to work at accepting myself as I am and moving toward a greater level of health for myself. I can't change who I am until I accept myself *as* I am.

God, I accept my failures and shortcomings, my doubts and manipulative behavior. Help me grow along with him as we both reach for a new quality of life. Amen.

NO MORE "SHOULDING"

Someone constantly used "should" on me. I used it myself when no one else did. I lived my life by what I "should," "ought," or "must" be doing.

Those three words never gave me a choice because they dictated my actions. When my emotions didn't correspond, a voice whispered, "You shouldn't feel that way," and I felt depressed for failing again.

I've determined to have no more "shoulding" in my life. "Should" says someone else is making choices for me. In my case, it's usually the voice of my father, long dead but as real as ever.

When I get frustrated, I hop into my car, close the windows, and scream, "No one is going to should on me today!" I feel a lot better afterward. I want to choose, and I'm learning to make decisions. It's not easy for me to shut out that "shoulding" voice but I'm doing it. The more I succeed, the better I feel.

Almighty God, help me so that I don't lose sight of my needs as I push the "should" out of my life. Amen.

I DON'T LIKE HIM

I liked everybody and would do anything to help. If people seemed to need me, I rushed to the scene.

I never thought about whether I liked them. Doesn't the Bible tell us we're supposed to like everybody? I grew up believing that as a good Christian I must love my neighbor. I could never acknowledge that I failed to love someone.

One day I talked with a former narcotics abuser who spends a lot of time with my husband. As he talked, I heard myself saying internally, I don't like him. After that experience, I began to realize that many people have passed through my life whom I didn't like. I now understand I don't have to like everybody. I couldn't, even if I tried.

God of love, instead of my trying to love everybody, help me to be more faithful to those I can and do love. Amen.

HANDS OFF!

Until I explained, the children laughed at my hand-printed signs around the house. They all read, HANDS OFF! Their mother is addicted to prescription drugs. I spent years trying to cure her and it never worked. Now I'm trying this simple plan I call Hands Off.

She is responsible for herself. I can't solve her problems because they aren't mine to solve. Worrying about her doesn't help either. When she creates her own disaster, I allow her to face the consequences.

"I'm giving you freedom," I told her, "freedom to be who you are, to be responsible for your actions. I love you and I'll be here for you—but I have taken my hands off."

Those were hard words to say but I've stuck with them, despite the painful agony of yearning to take over again.

God, give me daily strength to keep my hands off and to keep on loving her. Amen.

REJECTING REJECTIONS

I wanted everyone to like me. When they didn't, I suffered rejection. When they criticized, I interpreted that as rejection. When he relapsed, not only did I see that as his hurting himself but also as his turning against me and my love for him. I was so set up for rejection that I discovered it in almost every conversation or incident in my life.

I'm handling things differently since I decided to reject rejection. When he criticizes my cooking, I remind myself that he is stating a food preference, he is not rejecting me. If he doesn't like a particular dress I wear, he is indicating his choice. That is not rejection.

When anyone rejects me—and it does happen—I say, "That hurts." But my pain doesn't mean I'm worthless or bad. Others may not value me, but that's only their opinion.

God, it's your opinion that counts. Thanks for endowing me with worth. Amen.

FIRST PRIORITY

Here are three instances of priorities.

First, at a time-management seminar we learned about listing priorities. The leader pounded into us, "Your first priority is yourself. Get yourself straight, and you can handle the rest."

Second, when I ran high school track, the coach used to tell us to get plenty of sleep, eat nutritious food, and not to worry. "If you take care of your body and mind, the running takes care of itself."

Third, in a TV drama a doctor faced an emergency operation. He carefully washed his hands. When the husband yelled at him to hurry, he answered, "This comes first. Otherwise my efforts aren't worth much."

Setting priorities helps to determine our actions. Number one for me is: I am only responsible for me.

I can now think differently about her and her problem. I'm supportive, but she is not my first concern.

God, teach me the true priorities in life and help me stay with them. Amen.

TAKING IT PERSONALLY

"You're a weird lady," he said in one of our fights. "I get high and you get depressed."

"If you loved me," I said, "you'd throw away your drugs."

"What's my love for you got to do with it?"

I don't remember the rest of the argument— we had so many. But that day I heard an important statement. His drugs have nothing to do with his love or commitment to me.

When I talked this over with a group, one of them pointed out that he is a victim of a compulsive behavior. He will continue to abuse drugs until he gets the appropriate treatment. Then she said, "He isn't saying he doesn't love *you* when he gets high. He's saying he doesn't love himself."

Now I can laugh at the things I once took personally. This attitude made as much sense as accepting blame for the days when the sun didn't shine.

Loving God, help me realize that I don't have to take his—or anybody's—actions as personal rejection or dislike of me. Amen.

HE MADE ME DO IT

I keep hearing songs that complain because someone *made* the singer love or hate or go astray. How wrong those lyrics are! None of us *makes* anybody love us.

I applied that truth to various situations in my life. I used to say to her, "You make me angry." Or, "You're driving me crazy." Now I know better. I reacted to her. I *allowed* her to upset me.

I still feel angry, anxious, afraid, outraged, rejected, ashamed, confused, and dozens of other emotions. They are *my* emotions, and I am responsible for how I respond to them.

This reminds me of the time I saw a small boy trip over a chair leg. He kicked the chair and said, "Naughty. You made me fall down." My reactions to life's situations made about as much sense. I can no longer blame anyone outside myself.

God, help me to stop blaming others for "making" me feel bad. Amen.

FORGIVING ME

I grew up hearing, "Don't stay angry or carry grudges. You must forgive." While I sometimes had trouble forgiving, I knew it was the right thing to do.

What didn't become clear to me until recently was the need to forgive myself. When I failed or made mistakes, I cringed inside. I lectured myself. *You failed again, just like always. Don't you ever do anything right?*

Nobody acted more harshly toward me than I did against myself. I picked up on the slightest flaw and filled my mind with my own inadequacy.

While it's been difficult, I have been moving closer toward unconditionally accepting myself as worthwhile. I respect my needs and work toward meeting them. The biggest obstacle, however, still lies in forgiving myself. I am now showing myself kindness, and that includes self-forgiveness as I pray daily.

Our Father, forgive me my trespasses as I learn to forgive myself. Amen.

POSTMORTEMS

I use the postmortem approach when I can't prevent unpleasant and disruptive things from happening, no matter how hard I try. Afterward I examine all the facts to figure out what went wrong. Sometimes I can piece things together clearly. On other occasions I have to go to my support group or my therapist. They help me clear my thoughts and calm my emotions.

Here are three rules I've set up in doing postmortems:

1. I take responsibility for my feelings.
2. I allowed myself to feel this way.
3. Nobody made me feel this way.

Then I can ask myself questions to get at why I reacted as I did.

Once I understand my reactions, I can fortify myself by taking preventive measures.

God, help me to understand past reactions so I can avoid similar mistakes in the future. Amen.

SEEING THE LIGHT

When he called me a crusader, I flew into a rage. "Out to reform the whole world," he accused. I tried to explain I only wanted him to change, but he never listened to that part.

He was partially right. I was like a misguided evangelist—filled with zeal but lacking wisdom.

I used to be so sure that if he would listen long enough I could set him straight and he'd change. After fifteen years of nagging, blaming, pleading, and screaming, I had a moment of light—of insight—that helped me straighten out my thinking. No matter how much I want him to be different, I have no control over his choices. I can't make him understand anything he doesn't want to know.

Wise God, thanks for helping me to see the light. Now help me to live with this insight. Amen.

LETTING GO

"For every one of us there comes a time to let go," the therapist said.

I fought against that advice. I didn't want to stop loving her. I don't have to tolerate her abuse either.

One night I faced myself squarely and said, "I've done everything I know to do. I'm afraid of what will happen, but I have to take that chance and let go."

Letting go means admitting to myself that she may never be drug-free. But in letting go I don't abandon her. I merely allow her to be a person who makes her own choices. She must choose her addiction or her freedom, and only she can do it.

God, I still claw at the air, trying to latch on, but I can't. I have let go, and I don't ever want to hold her down again. With your help I won't. Amen.

JUST PLAIN TIRED

I reached the limits of my ability. Too drained to care, too worn out to act, I said, "I can't keep carrying this burden."

Immediately guilt crept in and I heard myself whisper, "But he needs me. He's desperate. I can't quit now."

I made another foray and it was worse than ever. I lost my patience. I screamed at him. I had no peace. I would probably have kept it up if my son hadn't asked, "Mom, why are you angry all the time?"

I denied it then with more angry words, but he had gotten through to me. I *was* angry, and I had been angry all day. Suddenly I was exhausted. The battle seemed useless. Yet I couldn't give up. I responded by singing the only melody I knew. His words helped to change my tune.

Loving God, I'm learning new music now. I have switched to the major keys of compassion (for him and me) and understanding. Thanks for helping me abandon the minor keys. Amen.

MY PERSONAL DEMON

I didn't feel lovable. In rescuing her I settled for feeling needed and momentarily hid from myself the pain of who I was. By snatching her from the brink of hell, I fooled myself into thinking that I helped her. But I really was trying to help myself.

I did things like destroy her drugs or cut off her source—temporarily. Someone compared my action to the one pill the addict needs to feel better—momentarily.

Despite good intentions, I didn't help her win her battle against addiction. I kept trying to rescue her instead of allowing her to struggle through by herself.

It took me a long time to recognize what I call my personal demon: my own low sense of self-value. I rescued her because it made me feel worthwhile—briefly.

Now I know and I have exorcised my demon. Oddly enough, now that I'm better, so is she.

God, thank you for helping me to learn to like myself and to gain power over my personal demon of self-loathing. Amen.

FATAL ATTRACTION

I've had three husbands, and I tormented myself regularly with accusations. "You sure know how to pick them! Every one a loser." One was an alcoholic, another strung out on coke. The third showed no evidence of addiction when we met, but inwardly I think I knew. His problem involved prescription drugs—from at least thirty doctors.

I wasn't aware of choosing addicts as lovers. When I met each man, I felt immediately attracted. "I've fallen in love," I said.

I've since learned the reason for this fatal attraction: I have an uncanny ability to pick a needy person every time. Unconsciously, I choose him so I can take care of him, and yet I really want someone to take care of me. None of my husbands could take care of me, and I never let them care for themselves. It's late to try to change, but not too late. Now that I know the curse, I'm going to work for the cure—in me.

Caring God, help me overcome this fatal attraction. Amen.

MY ANSWERING QUESTION

I used to think my own needs weren't important. I didn't try to discover them because they wouldn't be met anyway. Or when a need tugged at me, I pushed it away, assuming it was wrong. Then I learned about meeting my needs and caring for *me,* but I didn't do anything because I didn't know how.

I'm different now. I have needs and a right to have them fulfilled. I also learned to ask myself a question that can lead me to an answer: "What do I need right now to take care of me?"

The answer doesn't always come easily. At times I've ignored or denied it. But by asking the question and through honest self-searching, I'm growing. I'm even learning to enjoy the process of admitting I have needs that are as important as those of any other human in the universe.

Loving God of all creation, help me to keep asking the question and listening to the answer. Amen.

WHERE'S GOD?

"God abandoned me a long time ago," I joked. "He's tied up taking care of everybody else." Although I smiled when I said these words, inwardly I believed what I said. Why wouldn't God give up on me? I thought. I'm a useless failure.

I can see now that it appeared God abandoned me because I abandoned myself. I didn't hear God speak because I didn't listen. I couldn't listen because I had so much pain.

My husband taught me from his Narcotics Anonymous experiences that God accepts us without conditions. Once I turned to God, I had someone to talk to who loved me and wanted only my good.

God is teaching me to be good to myself and to show me a little kindness. Although I sometimes get down on myself when I don't measure up, I know that God speaks to me through those needs and I'm learning to listen.

Caring God, thank you for speaking. Keep me listening always. Amen.

ACCEPTING GOD

For years I prayed for God to get her off those prescription drugs and make her the way she used to be. Every day I asked for a miracle, but none ever came. She got worse and I got angry at God.

For me, the turning back to God came when I accepted life as it was. Acceptance meant she might never recover, that she could walk out on me or perhaps die from an overdose. Once I faced life's realities, my anger toward God evaporated. God didn't change her; God helped me to change. Now I can cope with my day-by-day situation.

I got help for me, and I still pray that she will reach out too.

God, thank you for changing my attitudes to accept life's realities. Help her to change, too, by seeing her needs. Amen.

DECISIONS, DECISIONS

I didn't want to make the wrong decision—
and so I delayed choosing. A long time ago I
lost confidence in my ability to make choices.

I worried about what other people thought
even in simple matters like wearing a blue
skirt or a gray one. Each time I reached a
decision point, an inner voice asked, "But
what if . . . ?" I had to make perfect decisions. I allowed myself no mistakes without
heavy doses of guilt. When I made wrong
choices, someone in my family let me know.
At times it felt as if the future of the entire
planet depended on my decision.

Now I don't struggle quite as much. I say
aloud each day, "I am not perfect, so I don't
have to make perfect decisions." Or "In twen-
ty years, will this make any difference?"

*God, I don't want to abdicate making
choices, but I need your help in making them
wisely. Most of all, I need help just in making
them. Amen.*

IMPERFECT DECISIONS

I read that Babe Ruth struck out 1,330 times during his illustrious career. Today the newspapers show that the top batter in the National League has a .397 average. That means that out of ten trips to the plate, he strikes out two thirds of the time. That same man earns a million dollars a year.

When I read that, I decided I could live with imperfect decisions—that is, I could make mistakes. Actually I've made them all my life, but now I'm taking responsibility for them. To my surprise, they aren't so hard to handle. Allowing myself to fail without self-castigation makes life more enjoyable too.

God, help me accept that I don't have to make perfect decisions, only to do the best I can with the wisdom and knowledge available to me. And most of all, help me know it's okay to be wrong. Amen.

CLEAR THOUGHTS

We make the best decisions when we start with clear minds. That's the first of three rules I have set down for my own decision making. Instead of making a decision in the midst of confusion, I say to myself, I'll decide later when I'm mentally calm.

Second, I refuse to worry. I have learned that when I start getting anxious, I can halt my runaway worries. Telling myself "I will not allow that to trouble me and I will not tolerate worry" actually works. I may have to tell myself five times in a day, but it's effective.

Third, God helps me sort out my thinking. Because I believe God wants only the best for me, I pray for the inspiration to make wise decisions. I also ask God to help me solve my problems.

God, you're good to me, and I'm grateful for your help. Amen.

HEALTHY THOUGHTS

The wise man said we are what we think.* I used to fill my mind with unhealthy thoughts. I dwelt on my failures. I daydreamed that my wife overdosed. I constantly rehearsed the problems her drugs caused us. I filled my mind with petty and evil thoughts.

I'm changing, now I've discovered that I can choose what to think, even though it's not always easy.

When I catch myself saying "I can't," I correct it to "Yes I can!" I refuse to concentrate on what I don't know or can't do.

On a 3 by 5 card I wrote five statements: *I like myself. I am lovable. I have a healthy mind. I am getting better every day in every way. With God's help, I can do anything.*† I read these words aloud five times every morning and again in the evening. I am learning to believe them. After all, they are true.

God, thanks for helping me realize that I'm worthwhile because you created me. Amen.

---

*See Proverbs 23:7 (KJV).
†See Philippians 4:13.

FOUR

RECOVERY

PRESENT-MOMENT LIVING

I seldom thought of the present because I expended my energies either in trying to fix up the past or in looking toward the future with foreboding.

"Allow life to happen," a wise counselor said.

Sound advice, but I didn't know how to do that. I am a fixer by nature, and I worked at fixing up everything for everybody. The counselor didn't give up on me and wouldn't let me give up on myself. She taught me how to relinquish regrets over the past. She helped me overcome my fears for the future.

"Make the most of today," she said. "You don't have to do anything except live now, without backward or forward glances."

God, I'm living in the present. You freed me from past failures. You're ridding me of anxieties over the future. You're teaching me to live by Jesus' maxim, "Don't be anxious about tomorrow. God will take care of your tomorrow too. Live one day at a time."* Amen.

---

*Matthew 6:34.

EXPECTATIONS

I got angry listening to people talk about their future and what they were going to do in six months or a year. I couldn't project anything into the future. I felt so bogged down by her drug-dependency problems, I could only think that each day and every year would be much like the previous ones.

I accepted her problem so fully that I had no hope she would improve. "What's the use?" I found myself asking. "She won't ever be different."

One day I realized that *I* could change— regardless of what *she* did. I didn't have to stay trapped in never-ending cycles of pain.

Now I can think about the future and I'm happier. Occasionally, the quagmire threatens to engulf me again. But most of the time I'm learning to enjoy life while still caring about her.

Caring God, thank you for giving me hope when I didn't know where else to turn. Amen.

CAUSE AND CURE

Like hundreds of others who love a narcotic addict, we wanted to help our son. We were willing to do anything.

We kept trying to figure out a way to get him cured. We showed more love. We withdrew from him. We called every day or we didn't call for weeks. We moved up and down the scale of effort, and nothing worked.

One day I reached the end. I prayed and wept and groaned and railed against God for not showing me how to help him. Then a thought came to me: You didn't cause it. You can't cure it.

It was so obvious I wonder why we never saw it before. We still want our son free from his addiction, but we're impotent. We hope. We pray. We wait. But we can't cure him. As sad as that has been to face, it has taken a heavy load from us. Because he's not cured doesn't indict us for failing. We find comfort in knowing we did the best we knew how.

God, help us stop trying to cure what only you and he can accomplish. Amen.

DETACHING

"You think I can walk away from a woman I've tried to help all these years? You talk about detaching like cutting a coupon from a magazine," I said.

"Then you don't understand detachment," the group leader answered calmly. "You don't detach from the *person* but from the pain."

Slowly the meaning sunk in. I recalled that shortly after we met, I told her, "I'm getting attached to you."

My attachment became overinvolvement. I attached my mental energies to solving her addiction problem. I attached my emotions and became her rescuer whenever she got into trouble. I attached myself so tightly that she depended on me. "Don't ever leave me," she pleaded. "I need you."

Detaching was a hard battle because I encountered the barriers of guilt, failure, and chaos. But I did it!

God, thanks for teaching me that I can care more effectively when I am detached from her pain. Amen.

DETACHING WAYS

"Detach! Detach!" they said. "But detach in love." That's where I had the problem. I couldn't seem to blend detaching with loving. For me, to detach meant cutting myself off from him, no matter how much my friends assured me that it wasn't so.

One day, in a fit of anger, I cut him off and determined never to get back into the same trap again. When I explained what happened, one friend said, "It's wiser to do it in love, but better to do it in anger than to stay attached."

From my new perspective I scrutinized my motives and emotions. I haven't liked a lot of things I've learned about myself, but I've accepted them. In the process I've felt more compassion for him. I don't like the way I detached myself, but I do like the fact that I did it!

God, thanks for your help and daily presence as I continue to work through my remaining conflicts. Amen.

DETACHING REWARDS

The struggle to detach myself from her drained me for months. Now I have a deep sense of peace in my life—something I never experienced before. I can give my love to her without using it to control her behavior or trying to force her into something I want.

I'm living my own life without constant feelings of guilt. I still love her but I can honestly say, "I am not responsible for your actions."

I even laughed the other day when I realized that I was just minding my own business. I was taking care of me—a full-time job in itself. She has to learn to start taking charge of her own life. I have many high-energy days and enjoy being me. I have never been happier in my life.

I have detached myself not only from her problem but from my lifelong habit of taking care of other people.

Caregiving God, thank you for caring for me and freeing me. Help her. She's needy and I can't cure her. Amen.

H.O.W.?

"Sure, I believe in detaching, in letting go," I said. "Just one question: How do I do it?" I found the answer in the three-part formula H.O.W.*

First, *Honesty.* I must be honest about what I feel and what I'm doing. We all have clever ways of deceiving ourselves. I have to shine a strong searchlight on my motives and attitudes.

Second, *Openness.* For me that meant listening and admitting that I used unhealthy means of trying to solve problems. I had to learn to accept my failures and to accept my strengths too.

Third, *Willingness.* I had to want to try a different way of coping. This third step took the longest for me because it forced me to change my habitual patterns.

I learned H.O.W. and I learned how. It is now becoming a habitual response that replaces obsessive worrying and manipulating.

Wise God, I'm grateful for H.O.W. Help me to stick with it. Amen.

---

*See Melody Beattie, *Codependent No More* (Center City, Minn.: Hazelden Foundation, 1987).

TWO STEPS

"You only need two concepts to begin to change," a speaker told my sister. "Take those two steps, and you're walking in the right direction."

As I listened, the speaker helped me to see that I also needed to take those two steps. He called the first one awareness. I had denied her addiction. I lied to myself, thinking, Once she gets through this problem, she'll get a grip on herself. I had denied my co-dependency. Now I was aware of it.

The second step is acceptance. I learned to say, "My sister is an addict. I am a co-dependent. Both of us need help." Acceptance means admitting the truth but also refusing to allow either of us any excuses for our conditions.

The two steps didn't cure us; they did point us in the right direction. That's the real secret of growth—moving in the right direction.

God, thanks for pointing the way. Now give us both courage to follow. Amen.

THE WAY OUT

The past year has taken the heaviest emotional toll of my life. I faced myself and, in the process, began to feel my emotions again. I accepted my situation and vowed to have wholeness. Yet what a price it has cost!

When I became aware of my past behavior patterns, I wanted to run away. I didn't want to feel those heavy negative emotions.

"The way out is through," advised a friend. "You can't ignore or run away if you want to get better."

I held on, despite my fluctuating emotions. I struggled with rejection and loneliness. At times anger overwhelmed me, and I wanted to blame the whole world. I cried so often I wondered if the tears would ever stop. But I stayed with it and held on when I didn't think I could.

God, I'm on the way out of my co-dependency because you've helped me to go through. With your continued help, I'm going to make it. Amen.

SHE'S CURED

I wanted to believe she's cured, but past experiences made me skeptical.

"Dad," she said, "this time I've licked it for good." I must have heard that a dozen times. I wanted to believe she was cured, but she has left behind a path of destruction and pain. I wanted to trust her, and yet I thought, She'll have to prove herself first.

When she came home she didn't yell, "I'm cured!" She said, "Dad, I'm in recovery." At first I thought it was a new trick to lower my resistance. Then she talked about her confused feelings and how she realized the trouble she had brought to the family and to herself. That's when I embraced her, physically and emotionally.

She's not cured; she *is* in recovery. Both of us understand the difference. Instead of being a cause of worry, it offers me hope. She is facing reality. She knows the tenuousness of her situation.

God, she's not cured and maybe she never will lick this habit. But I thank you that she is recovering. Amen.

RECOVERY

"If he would only change," I must have said ten thousand times. "Nothing is going to happen until he recovers from his drug addiction."

I was wrong. I didn't have to wait for him to change. For the first time I admitted that I had become obsessed with "helping" him. Yet instead of help, I was caretaking. I faced things in myself I didn't like: self-hatred, anger, guilt, my weakness in being attracted to and tolerant of such behavior.

Facing was the first hard step. Growing beyond that has been a slow, often painful experience. I've had help from Narcotics Anonymous, my pastor, my friends. I can now say that I am becoming a whole person. And I like who I am becoming.

God, you still change people and enrich their lives. You're doing it for me as you've done it for others. Thank you. Amen.

WHY SHOULD I FEEL THIS WAY?

Now that she's in recovery, I feel as if I'm in recovery too. I'm recovering my zest for life and allowing myself to experience the normal flow of feelings.

Even so, I'm still grappling with my emotions. I keep asking myself, Why should I feel this way? Why did I blow up? Resent her? Blame her?

I finally mentioned this to my pastor. He said, "You can't live with a narcotic addict and not have it take its toll on you. Anyone bombarded by such destructive weapons is entitled to a lot of painful, negative feelings. I commend you for surviving."

Then he turned my question around. "Why *shouldn't* you feel this way? As long as you try to decide how you should or should not feel, you are in trouble. It's better if you allow the feelings to come and then ask, 'What is going on in me right now?'"

God, I feel my emotions. Help me to understand what I feel instead of asking why. Amen.

A LITTLE KICKING

Facing reality, especially for those of us involved with drug-dependent types, forces us to scrutinize ourselves. We don't take those steps without a little kicking, a lot of screaming, and an abundance of confusion.

I've been reading Elisabeth Kübler-Ross,* who identified five stages terminally ill people go through to conclude life with "a happy death." It made me realize how closely my path toward change paralleled these stages.

The steps are denial ("This can't be!"), anger ("Why did this happen to me?"), bargaining ("God, if you'll ——— then I'll ———"), depression ("What's the use?"), and acceptance ("It's all right").

I've been through those stages, some more than once. I now have the undeniable proof of inner tranquillity.

Wise God, thank you for putting up with my kicking, screaming, and doubting. Now help me accept whatever life brings to me. Amen.

———
*See Elisabeth Kübler-Ross, *On Death and Dying* (New York: Macmillan Co., 1969).

ANOTHER VIEW

A friend spoke of change as a threefold process. He said, "First you go through the forgiving phase. You forgive her and you forgive yourself."

The second phase, healing, slowly mends the brokenness and pain. This prepares us for the third phase: wholeness. Here we are open to God and to whatever life offers us.

The process sounds easier to put into effect than it is. For me it was painful, confusing, frustrating, and awkward. At times I felt I was falling apart and vacillated between shock and panic. I felt isolated, lonely, and vulnerable.

Yet I also experienced hope—sometimes exaggerated and euphoric, but still hope. During the painful weeks, I told myself, "This is not a normal process, but a necessary one. The turmoil will end."

God, I haven't quite made it but I'm on the way. Give me strength and encouragement for the rest of the journey. Amen.

FEELING MY FEELINGS

In our family, plagued with drug abuse, we couldn't face emotional honesty. We tacitly encouraged lying and dishonesty. We pretended the drugs weren't "really that bad." We covered up for his bizarre behavior. All that time I hurt deeply inside and felt vulnerable.

Vulnerability can be dangerous. Hurts piled upon hurt, and I felt that no one cared.

I withdrew, making myself an emotional zombie. I cut off my emotions to survive the pain. In doing so, I lost touch with the emotional part of me. A friend said, "You're fine except that you're oppressed, depressed, and repressed."

We made a joke out of it, but it told me someone else understood—and cared. Her words helped me start getting in touch with my feelings again.

God, you gave us the ability to feel. Help me to reclaim this ability, no matter how much it hurts. Amen.

A LITTLE KINDNESS

My relatives said harsh things about me, mostly behind my back. She had told them wild stories and said I drove her to drug dependency.

Yet they were no harder on me than I was on myself. I saw my failures and perhaps even magnified their significance. Indelibly imprinted in my memory is every infraction, careless word, and act of poor judgment. I didn't need more pointing fingers; I needed a little kindness.

One person shook his head after one of my recitals of failure. "You're too hard on yourself." When I protested he added, "You need more kindness in your life, and I hope you'll learn to give some to yourself and to accept it from others."

That was the beginning. I'm not nearly as demanding on myself as I used to be. I'm learning to put away my past mistakes and feel good when I do something right. I am going to keep getting better.

Kind and compassionate God, help me to show more kindness to me. Amen.

SOMEONE GREATER

"Let go," they urged. "Turn it over to God." Instead of God, they sometimes said "Higher Power" or "Jesus" or simply "the Lord."

"I don't know how," I protested. "I can't believe that God cares that much about me." I've had a hard struggle in letting go of all the inner turmoil we co-dependents struggle with. Having faith hasn't been easy. I have admitted that I need Someone Greater who knows *and cares.* I finally believe that God does care about what's happening to me and wants to help.

I can now say confidently, "I have faith. I believe in God who works through people and circumstances. I feel more secure and alive than ever."

Great God, you are Someone Greater. Unburden me and give me the inner strength to keep getting better. Amen.

PRIVATE RETREATS

Friends taught me the secret of private retreats. When chaos strikes, I now stop myself from reacting to the situation, regardless of how it started or who caused it.

I say and do as little as possible. I physically get out of the place as soon as possible. We call refusing to become entangled in destructive situations our "retreat to advance."

My friends have a variety of private retreats. One person meditates. Another reads the Bible or an inspirational book. One woman scrubs her kitchen floor. I like going for a long, fast walk. As long as it's not destructive behavior, the type of retreat doesn't matter.

I'm winning a lot of battles by retreating from situations where I couldn't win. By remaining in the situation, I set myself up for more heartbreak and turmoil.

Gracious God, I love my private retreats where I can be alone with you. These retreats make it easier to face life again. Amen.

ASKING HIM

I didn't know how to ask for anything for myself. I played games, hoping he would understand—such as hinting, manipulating, adding guilt and coercion. I did anything except come right out with "I need ———. Will you give it to me?"

Three months ago I needed to be held. A simple thing, and yet I couldn't work up the courage to ask him. For half an hour I struggled until I said, "Would you hold me in your arms a few minutes?" He smiled and put his arms around me.

That single experience has given me courage to ask. That's also part of learning to care for myself. Caring entails knowing what I want and providing it myself or asking for help. To ask does get easier as I admit that I'm worth caring about.

Magnificent God, I'm a needy person, like everyone else in the world. Thank you for helping me ask for what I need. Amen.

ARMING MYSELF

I'm learning to fortify myself so that I am ready when I have to face my battles. I'm even learning to see conflicts coming. By being ready I can choose how to respond: I can retreat, fight, or detach. I don't have to allow myself to be victimized again and again.

When I face a potential crisis I ask myself, What do I need to do to take care of me? Do I need to shut up? Walk out? Let it go? Assert myself?

I now get caught less often in pain-and-loss situations. I'm learning skills that defuse wars before they start. This has turned out to be more simple than I had imagined. It helps me know that I don't have to control situations. I do have to be on guard and ready to take care of me.

Heavenly Guardian, it means a lot that you're here to protect me from destructive actions. I'm gaining strength all the time. Amen.

MY BEST FRIEND

I never had many friends, and I wasn't sure I wanted any. Friends failed. They hurt me and brought me pain (or at least I blamed them for much of my pain).

I finally decided I wanted friends, no matter what. Someone defined a friend as "a person who knows everything about you and still loves you." Who knows more about me than I do? I didn't try to develop relationships with others until I worked out my own inner need. I decided to become my own best friend.

While I will always need other people, I am my personal therapist, confidant, spiritual adviser, partner, *and* best friend. I am being all these things to myself—and enjoying the excitement of learning more about me.

God, you're the only one who enables me to be my best friend. Thank you for helping me to like this friend. Amen.

CONGRATULATIONS!

"You did a great job," I said. "You planned, worked hard, and pulled it off. Congratulations."

I said those words to myself. A year ago I would never have even thought of them. I didn't compliment others easily and would *never* have been able to affirm my own actions. Now I can and I do!

Part of learning to care for myself has involved self-acceptance. I do some things well; a few things I do exceptionally well. When people accomplish their goals, they need encouragement. Compliments go a long way in showing appreciation. If I can say, "Congratulations for a job well done" to others, I can say those same words to myself. I need to hear them too.

Loving God, thank you for helping me affirm myself and appreciate the things I do well. Amen.

NO-FAULT LIVING

Before I embraced no-fault living, I allowed myself to be tricked into doing things that hurt me. I've stopped doing that, and I've stopped refusing to blame others for their failures.

Things like manipulating, rescuing, and care-taking are my problems. *They are not me.* I refuse to pick on myself. I no longer allow self-accusation to depress me.

I am lovable, and I am worth getting to know. I have been able to say, How clever of people to choose a wonderful friend like me! I'm not a second-class citizen, and I don't lead a secondhand life filled with second-best relationships.

When I fail (and I do), I accept it as a part of being human. I forgive myself and ask God to help me not to fail again.

Helper God, I'm learning no-fault living. Help me to realize how great life can be for all of us who live no-fault lives. Amen.

THE SECOND COMMANDMENT

Jesus said that the greatest commandment is to love God totally. The second is to love others *in the same way that we love ourselves.*

I wanted to ignore the implied portion of the second commandment—self-love. I didn't like anything I did and felt ashamed of being me. I didn't like my body, my abilities, my personality. Someone was always brighter or more talented. My opinions didn't matter.

I constantly said demeaning things to others and myself: "I'm a jerk." "I never remember names."

That's changing now—slowly. I am valuing myself as a person, and doing so helps me value others. Now I understand how the second commandment works. The more loving I am toward myself, the more loving I become toward others. I can't separate loving myself from loving others. We're all created by a loving God, and all of us are worthwhile.

Wise and caring God, thanks for teaching me to value myself and others. Amen.

BEAUTIFUL PEOPLE

"They're the beautiful people," a woman said. In her vocabulary, that term distinguished them from ordinary folk. As I understand her words, she meant they like themselves and affirm their value. Their true inner beauty shines through.

The beautiful people perceive themselves as wholesome and healthy and allow others to see their true selves bursting forth. They don't berate themselves or focus on failures and flaws.

Despite our differences in income, success, and outward beauty, we're all about the same. We're human. We are all part of the beautiful people. We just have to claim our membership.

I've decided to take my place alongside the beautiful people. I'm one of them. It's what we tell ourselves and what we believe about ourselves that count.

Beautiful God, thank you for making me one of the beautiful people—and thank you for helping me believe it. Amen.

GENTLE PERMISSION

I survived my own emotional grief. Many days I didn't know if I would. Some days I didn't care. "Will I always have this much pain?" I asked.

I talked to myself often: "I'm giving you permission to go through this, but be gentle with me." That helped me in going through periods when I felt drained, inadequate, and emotionally off balance.

I had outside help, too. A few friends let me talk and talk and talk. One of them, like me, is married to a woman addicted to illegal drugs. He had been through it himself, and he helped immensely.

God touched me when I reached into the darkness for a helping hand. I learned the Serenity Prayer as used by Narcotics Anonymous and other groups. I have said it so often it has become second nature to me:

God grant me the serenity to accept the things I cannot change, courage to change the things I can, and wisdom to know the difference. Amen.

NECESSARY LOSSES

Recovery brings losses. As he continues to recover, I have to make changes too. Our relating patterns are in flux. On the whole, I'd call them positive changes. That doesn't make them easier to accept.

My head reminds me that he is changing—improving—because he is recovering from narcotic dependency. My heart says he's better, but he is also deliberately harassing me and maliciously hurting me. Nothing I depended on is stable, and I'm emotionally off balance. I've lost the comfort, the known factor of our relationship. I hated him for being the way he was, but at least there was a certain predictability to it.

I want to face these changes, and I find it helpful to think of them as necessary losses. He's becoming stronger, healthier, and happier. I want to adjust, to encourage him to recover. While I face the reality of loss of predictability, I know we have a chance to build together on a firmer foundation.

God, help me accept these changes and be grateful. Amen.

HOLD THAT THOUGHT!

Now aware of my emotions, I allow myself to feel them. I'm making conscious decisions about how to express negative feelings. Recently I've become aware of the repeating patterns in my life. I can see that I got myself into unpleasant situations, painfully extricated myself, only to slide back into the same ruts again.

I felt rejection again when she refused to talk all day. I thought about the hurt I experienced and decided to treat her with silence as well.

Then it hit me: That's the pattern I always used. Whoever spoke first lost the game. It seemed natural to respond that way again. That's when I mentally said, Oh, oh, hold that thought. I went to her and said, "I'm sorry if you're upset. I hope it's not over something I did."

"Just angry at myself," she said. She smiled at me, and I knew I had broken the pattern.

God, make me aware of the old patterns and help me find the right way to handle new situations. Amen.

DISCUSS IT

Discuss how I'm feeling? Six months ago that seemed crazy. What good would it do? Who wants to hear about me anyway?

I had tried talking to my husband but it never worked. A friend advised, "Don't try to reason with him when he's high. You only set yourself up for more anger."

She helped me see that I needed to talk about my feelings in a calm situation with someone I trusted. When I do this, I can usually figure out an appropriate way to express my emotions. Talking helps diffuse my anger. Instead of acting rashly, I pause to figure out what I'm actually feeling.

I ask, "What do I need from that person?" Once I figure out the answer, I can go to that person and express it. If it's my husband, and he's high, I wait until we can discuss things quietly.

God, life is getting better because I'm getting better. Thank you for being with me through all of this. Amen.

SET THE GOAL

For the past eight years my goal was just to make it through that day. My wife is addicted to prescription drugs. I woke up each morning and pleaded, "God, help me to make it today."

Once I became aware of my narrow limits, I started setting broader goals. Not only did I find it hard to get started, but I had hundreds of doubts about my capabilities. I discovered immense help by saying to God, "I can't do everything in the world, but I don't know my limits until I set goals and try to reach them."

I can decide what I want in life and plan to stretch toward achieving them. By setting goals, I'm feeling an uplift in spirit. Now I have a purpose in life and a sense of direction.

God, my hand is in yours. I know I have not yet begun to touch the limits of my abilities or desires. Keep me reaching. Amen.

PAPER GOALS

Once I started setting goals, I repeated them aloud to myself. An expert urged, "Write your goals on paper. The discipline enables you to state them clearly and concisely. It also has the effect of reinforcing your commitment to them." I've been writing my goals under two headings: the easy goals and the long-range ones.

As my first goal I wrote, *I will not scream at him today.* It took me a week to make it through a whole day. Now it has become almost second nature, and I'm past the screaming stage.

When writing my long-range goals, I pray for wisdom and ask for divine strength to accomplish them.

God, I offer you my goals and submit myself to you. Strengthen me as I strive for fulfillment. Guide me when my goals need revision. Amen.